THE OFFICIAL
ENGLAND
ANNUAL 2023

Written by Andy Greeves
Designed by Daniel Brawn

A Grange Publication

© 2022. Published by Grange Communications Ltd., Edinburgh, under licence from The Football Association.

Printed in the EU.

ISBN 978-1-915295-45-3

WELCOME TO THE OFFICIAL ENGLAND ANNUAL 2023

What a year 2022 was for England as the Lionesses won the UEFA Women's European Championships to secure their first major trophy success, while the Three Lions took part in their 16th FIFA World Cup in Qatar.

There were big competitions for other England teams too. Ian Foster's Young Lions took part in the 2022 UEFA U19 European Championship while England Cerebral Palsy team scored an impressive 21 goals in six matches at the 2022 IFCPF World Cup.

2023 promises to be just as hectic a year as 2022 was, with Sarina Wiegman's Lionesses having all but secured a place at the year's FIFA Women's World Cup at the time of writing. Meanwhile, Gareth Southgate's side begin their qualification campaign for UEFA Euro 2024 in March 2023.

In the Official England Annual 2023, we profile the players who currently make up England's Men's and Women's senior squads. We take a look back on the Lionesses' triumphant UEFA Euro 2022 campaign and we check out how the Three Lions got on in their fixtures in the run-up to the 2022 FIFA World Cup. There are also historic features on the first international football match - which saw England take on Scotland in 1872 - 50 years of the Lionesses and the 100-year anniversary of football being staged at Wembley Stadium for the first time.

Elsewhere, there are other features, quizzes, games and plenty more besides to entertain England fans of all ages!

COME ON ENGLAND!

#THREELIONS #LIONESSES

CONTENTS

EURO · EUROPEAN CHAMPIONS · STARS

England Women's victory at the European Championships in the summer of 2022 put an end to 56 years of hurt. The last time the Three Lions or Lionesses won a major, senior trophy was back in 1966, when the men's team lifted the World Cup.

The Lionesses sealed their UEFA Euro 2022 triumph after a stunning 2-1 extra-time victory over eight-time winners Germany in the final on 30 July, thanks to goals from Ella Toone and Chloe Kelly. They won all their group games, including an 8-0 thumping of Norway while they beat Spain and Sweden in the knockout phase on the way to the Wembley final, which was played in front of a record crowd for a European Championship Final.

Sarina Wiegman's side conceded just two goals throughout the whole tournament and netted 22 times. Six of those goals came from Beth Mead, who picked up the Golden Boot and Player of the Tournament award.

ENGLAND 1-0 AUSTRIA

6 JULY 2022
OLD TRAFFORD, MANCHESTER

ENGLAND: Earps, Bronze, Bright, Williamson, Daly, Stanway, Walsh, Mead (Kelly 64), Kirby (Toone 63), Hemp, White (Russo 64)

AUSTRIA: Zinsberger, Wienroither, Wenninger, Schnaderbeck (Georgieva 77), Hanshaw; Puntigam, Dunst, Zadrazil, Feiersinger (Höbinger 87), Naschenweng (Hickelsberger-Füller 59), Billa

ATTENDANCE:
68.871

A first-half goal from Mead got England off to a winning start at UEFA Women's Euro 2022 as the Lionesses beat Austria 1-0. The winger chested down Fran Kirby's pass and, finding space inside the box, lifted the ball over Arsenal team-mate Manuela Zinsberger in the Austria goal on 16 minutes. A VAR check was done to ensure the ball had fully crossed the line, and the goal stood.

The Lionesses had chances to double their lead against the semi-finalists from Euro 2017 but Ellen White headed wide and Zinsberger deflected Lauren Hemp's effort over the bar just before half-time. Wiegman's side remained on top for much of the second half with Austria's best chance coming with 10 minutes to go when England keeper Mary Earps was called into action, diving to her left to push away a Barbara Dunst strike.

68,871 fans watched the Lionesses' victory at Old Trafford - a then-record crowd for a European Women's Championship game.

ENGLAND 8-0 NORWAY

11 JULY 2022
AMEX STADIUM, BRIGHTON

ENGLAND: Earps, Bronze, Bright, Williamson, Daly (Greenwood 57), Stanway (Scott 80), Walsh, Kirby (Toone 57), Mead, White (Russo 57), Hemp (Kelly 70)

Norway: Pettersen, T. Hansen, Mjelde, Thorisdottir, Blakstad, Bøe Risa (Maanum 59), Syrstad Engen, Sævik (Bergsvand 46), Graham Hansen (Eikeland 75), Reiten (Terland 84), Hegerberg (Bizet Ildhusøy 75)

ATTENDANCE:
28.847

England ran riot against Norway in Brighton, recording their biggest-ever win at a European Championships and progressing to the knockout stages of the tournament in the process. Georgia Stanway slotted in a 12th-minute penalty for the Lionesses' opener after White was fouled in the box, before Hemp doubled their lead with a back-heeled effort, three minutes later.

White netted just before the half-hour mark to make it three and Mead headed in her first of the night in the 34th minute before adding another just moments later, when she rolled the ball past Guro Pettersen in the Norway goal. White bagged her brace before the break to move to within one goal of Wayne Rooney's combined all-time England goalscoring record.

Alessia Russo came off the bench to score her first England goal on 66 minutes. Mead claimed her hat-trick to round off a record-breaking evening. It was the first time a team has ever scored eight goals in a match at a Women's Euros and the victory marked a statement of intent from Wiegman's side.

ENGLAND 5-0 NORTHERN IRELAND

15 JULY 2022
ST MARY'S STADIUM. SOUTHAMPTON

ENGLAND: Earps, Bronze (Carter 74), Bright (Greenwood 46), Williamson, Daly, Stanway (Toone 46), Walsh, Mead, Kirby, Hemp (Kelly 60), White (Russo 46)

NORTHERN IRELAND: Burns, McKenna, Nelson (Hutton 87), McFadden, Vance, Rafferty (Burrows 66), Callaghan (Wilson 87), Furness (Caldwell 80), Holloway (Magee 66), Wade, K. McGuinness

ATTENDANCE:
30.785

The Lionesses put five past Northern Ireland as they completed their group stage fixtures in style. England were without Head Coach Wiegman at St Mary's after she tested positive for Covid-19. Her side dominated possession from kick-off but it wasn't until the 40-minute mark that Chelsea's Kirby broke the deadlock with a brilliant strike into the top corner.

Right before half-time, Mead doubled England's lead with her fifth goal of the tournament and Russo headed home the Lionesses' third goal just after the break with her first touch after coming off the bench. Four minutes later, it was four for England and another for Russo, who hit her finish well beyond Northern Ireland keeper Jackie Burns.

Their fifth and final goal of the night came courtesy of an own goal from Northern Ireland defender Kelsie Burrows who deflected Mead's shot into her own net to ensure England topped Group A without conceding a goal. Northern Ireland, who were competing in their first women's major tournament, finished bottom of the group.

FINAL GROUP A TABLE

		P	W	D	L	GF	GA	GD	PTS
1	ENGLAND (Q)	3	3	0	0	14	0	+14	9
2	AUSTRIA (Q)	3	2	0	1	3	1	+2	6
3	NORWAY	3	1	1	2	4	10	−6	3
4	NORTHERN IRELAND	3	0	1	3	1	11	−10	0

QUARTER-FINAL

ENGLAND 2-1 SPAIN (AET)

20 JULY 2022
AMEX STADIUM, BRIGHTON

ENGLAND: Earps, Bronze, Bright, Williamson, Daly (Greenwood 82); Stanway, Walsh (Scott 116), Kirby (Toone 64), Mead (Kelly 58), White (Russo 58), Hemp (Parris 116)

SPAIN: Paños, Batlle, Paredes, Mapi León, Carmona, Bonmatí, Guijarro, Abelleira (Aleixandri 70), Cardona (Del Castillo 46), González (S. García 77), Caldentey (Sarriegi 100)

ATTENDANCE:
28.994

England Women booked their place in the semi-finals after a hard-fought, extra-time 2-1 victory over Spain. The Lionesses were the first to have the ball in the back of the net, but White's goal on 37 minutes was ruled out with Lucy Bronze ruled offside in the build-up.

Spain kept up the pressure and Wiegman's women conceded their first goal of the tournament on 54 minutes when Esther González hit the target for Spain from a Del Castillo cross. As the minutes ticked by, it started to look like England could be on their way out... But substitute Ella Toone equalised six minutes from time with a close-range volley to take the game into extra-time – much to the delight of the England crowd in Brighton.

The Lionesses had the impetus they needed to go on and win the match and Georgia Stanway struck a brilliant 96th-minute winner from long-range to send them through to their fourth successive semi-final in major tournaments – they also reached this stage at the 2015 and 2019 FIFA Women's World Cups and the 2017 Euros.

SEMI-FINAL

ENGLAND 4-0 SWEDEN

26 JULY 2022
BRAMALL LANE. SHEFFIELD

ENGLAND: Earps, Bronze, Bright, Williamson, Daly (Greenwood 86), Stanway (Scott 86), Walsh, Mead (Kelly 86), Kirby (Toone 79), Hemp, White (Russo 57)

SWEDEN: Lindahl, Ilestedt (Andersson 55), Sembrant (Bennison 76), Eriksson, Glas; Angeldal (Seger 51), Asllani, Björn, Rolfö, Blackstenius (Hurtig 76), Jakobsson (Rytting Kaneryd 51)

ATTENDANCE:
28.624

A cheeky Russo back-heel helped England through to the final, after they beat Sweden 4-0 in front of a sell-out crowd in Sheffield. Wiegman chose the same starting XI as in all their previous Lionesses matches at the competition and Mead opened the scoring on 34 minutes - her sixth of the tournament - when she turned in Bronze's cross.

It was roles reversed shortly after the break when Bronze headed in from Mead's corner.
Sweden kept pushing, but England were able to deal with everything thrown at them and Russo's outrageous back-heel, which went through the legs of Hedvig Lindahl in the Sweden goal on 68 minutes, effectively settled the tie at Bramall Lane. England weren't finished though and Kirby's lob with quarter of an hour remaining made it four, as the Lionesses booked their place in the final in style.

FINAL

ENGLAND 2-1 GERMANY (AET)

31 JULY 2022
WEMBLEY STADIUM. LONDON

ENGLAND: Earps, Bronze, Bright, Williamson, Daly (Greenwood 88), Stanway (Scott 88), Walsh, Mead (Kelly 64), Kirby (Toone 56), Hemp (Parris 120), White (Russo 56)

GERMANY: Frohms, Gwinn, Hendrich, Hegering (Doorsoun 103) Rauch (Lattwein 113) Magull (Dallmann 90), Oberdorf, Däbritz (Lohmann 73), Huth, Schüller (Anyomi 67) Brand (Wassmuth 45)

ATTENDANCE:
87.192

More than 87,000 people packed into Wembley Stadium to watch England take on Germany - the largest ever crowd for a European Championship final.

Manchester City striker White missed a couple of chances for the Lionesses in the first half and it was the Germans who came closest to breaking the deadlock on 25 minutes after a goalmouth scramble from a corner, but England keeper Earps pounced on the ball and held on tight.

It was 0-0 at the break and Wiegman made two changes early in the second half, bringing on Toone and Russo. Their impact was almost instant and when Toone, running onto a through ball from Keira Walsh, beautifully lobbed the ball over Germany keeper Merle Frohms on 62 minutes, Wembley erupted.

Germany nearly equalised four minutes later when Lina Magull's shot hit the crossbar, and she finally made the difference in the 79th minute, side-footing home at Earps' near post to force the game into extra-time.

It was another super substitute that provided the perfect finish for England though, as 24-year-old Chloe Kelly came off the bench to poke home the winner at the second attempt in the 110th minute, to give the Lionesses their first major tournament triumph and a place in the history books.

Wiegman also became the first manager to win back-to-back titles with two different nations as she also led the Netherlands to glory at UEFA Euro 2017.

GARETH SOUTHGATE

BIGGEST WIN

13-0 v IRELAND (A)

18 FEBRUARY 1882

ENGLAND SENIOR

MOST CAPS

125

PETER SHILTON

17 FIFA WORLD CUP APPEARANCES*

BEST PERFORMANCE   WINNERS   1966**

1 UEFA NATIONS LEAGUE FINAL TOURNAMENT APPEARANCE

BEST PERFORMANCE | THIRD PLACE | 2019

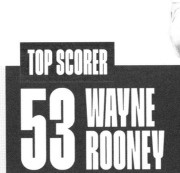

FIRST INTERNATIONAL
0-0 v SCOTLAND (A)
30 NOVEMBER 1872

TOP SCORER
53 WAYNE ROONEY

MEN'S PROFILE

10 UEFA EUROPEAN CHAMPIONSHIP APPEARANCES

BEST PERFORMANCE | RUNNERS-UP | 2020

HARRY KANE
CAPTAIN

*Figure includes England appearance at the 2022 FIFA World Cup

** The outcome of the 2022 FIFA World Cup was not known at the time of writing

GARETH SOUTHGATE   MANAGER

England's UEFA Nations League clash with Italy on 23 September 2022 marked Gareth Southgate OBE's 75th match as Three Lions Manager. Only Sir Bobby Robson, Sir Alf Ramsey and Sir Walter Winterbottom have taken charge of more England matches since The Football Association made the decision to appoint their first manager in 1946 (the England team was previously selected and overseen by the International Select Committee).

With the 2022 FIFA World Cup set to be Southgate's seventh as either a player or a manager, he has experienced reaching the last four at three previous major competitions – as a player at UEFA Euro 1996 and as manager at the 2018 FIFA World Cup and the delayed UEFA Euro 2020, when he guided England to the final.

Southgate is a product of Crystal Palace's youth system – a club he went on to represent for seven years at first team level and for whom he first captained at the age of just 23. His playing career later took him to Aston Villa and Middlesbrough where he won the Football League Cup at both. His senior England debut – the first of 57 caps – came as a substitute in a friendly against Portugal in December 1995.

D.O.B: 3 September 1970
Place of Birth: Watford
England Men's Manager
Since: September 2016

Southgate's managerial career began at Middlesbrough in June 2006. Despite not having the required coaching badges at the time, Southgate was granted an exemption to take the job and he guided Middlesbrough to two midtable Premier League finishes before departing the Riverside Stadium in October 2009. After four years in football punditry, Southgate became England U21s manager in 2013 and was in charge when the Young Lions won the Toulon Tournament in 2016.

Replacing Sam Allardyce as England's Manager in September 2016 – initially on an interim basis - Southgate was appointed permanently two months later, when he put pen-to-paper on a four-year contract. At the 2018 FIFA World Cup, the Three Lions reached the semi-final of the tournament, triumphing in a penalty shootout against Colombia along the way – the first time an England team has ever won a match on penalties at a World Cup.

Under Southgate, England topped their UEFA Nations League Group in 2019 and two years later, enjoyed a memorable run to the final of the delayed UEFA Euro 2020 with victories over Croatia, Czech Republic, Germany, Ukraine and Denmark along the way. He signed a new contract in November 2021 to take charge of England through until December 2024.

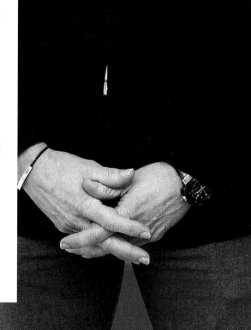

STEVE HOLLAND   ASSISTANT MANAGER

Steve Holland turned out for the likes of Derby County, Bury, Northwich Victoria and Swedish side Husqvarna FF during his playing career, but he had to retire through injury at the age of just 21. A year later, he became a youth coach at Crewe Alexandra, where he stayed for 17 years. Holland spent his last year at Gresty Road as the Railwaymen's manager, before spending a couple of months coaching at Stoke City. In 2009, he was snapped up by Chelsea, who handed him the role of managing their reserves.

Holland's two years with the Blues' culminated in him winning the Premier Reserve League and he eventually became involved with the first team as assistant manager to André Villas-Boas. Holland remained in the role for six years, working under the likes of Rafa Benítez, José Mourinho and Antonio Conte. He was also assistant manager when Roberto di Matteo's Chelsea won the Champions League in 2012.

In 2013, he became Gareth Southgate's assistant at England U21s, fulfilling that job alongside his Stamford Bridge commitments. He left Chelsea in 2017 to focus on England's senior team as assistant manager.

PAUL NEVIN   FIRST TEAM COACH

Paul Nevin returned to the England senior men's coaching staff in August 2021, having previously worked with the Three Lions from October 2018 through until the end of the 2019 UEFA Nations League campaign.

Nevin began his coaching career with Fulham's academy before going on to work with New Zealand Knights, Aspire Academy in Qatar, Norwich City and Brighton & Hove Albion. He took up a coaching role with West Ham United in February 2020 and a successful period for the Hammers has followed, with the club achieving their highest league finish for 22 years in 2020/21. He will continue in his role at the London Stadium full-time while working for England on a part-time basis.

CHRIS POWELL   FIRST TEAM COACH

Chris Powell played as a left-back for Southend United and Charlton Athletic amongst others in a lengthy 23-year playing career. He also appeared five times for England in the early 2000s. An experienced manager for Huddersfield Town and Southend United, he has worked as a first-team coach for England since 2019 and was assistant manager at Tottenham Hotspur in 2021, working under Spurs' temporary boss Ryan Mason.

MARTYN MARGETSON   GOALKEEPING COACH

Former Wales international Martyn Margetson played for the likes of Manchester City, Bolton Wanderers and Cardiff City in a senior career that spanned 15 years. Thereafter, he became a goalkeeping coach, representing a number of clubs including Cardiff, West Ham United and Crystal Palace while he worked with the Wales national team between 2011 and 2016. In 2016, Margetson joined the England national team as goalkeeping coach, continuing club duties with Everton and, since 2019, Swansea City. Martyn was England's goalkeeping coach during the 2018 FIFA World Cup, when the Three Lions won a World Cup penalty shootout for the first time.

MEN'S SENIOR TEAM

(H) Home (A) Away (N) Neutral Venue

*Information correct as of August 2022

GOALKEEPERS

JORDAN PICKFORD

AARON RAMSDALE

NICK POPE

Date/Place of Birth:
7 March 1994 - Washington
England Debut: 10 November
2017 v Germany (H)

Five shy of 50 England
appearances at the time of
writing, Jordan has been a Three
Lions regular since making his
senior international debut in
2017. Jordan featured in all
690 minutes of England's UEFA
Euro 2020 campaign, keeping
five clean sheets – more than
any other goalkeeper at the
competition. He also excelled at
the 2018 FIFA World Cup and
made a memorable save from
Carlos Bacca to help his country
to their first-ever World Cup
penalty shootout success against
Colombia in the tournament's
round of 16.

Date/Place of Birth:
14 May 1998 - Stoke-on-Trent
England Debut: 15 November
2021 v San Marino (A)

Capped at U18, U20 and U21 level
prior to making his senior debut,
Aaron started all five England
U19 matches which saw them
win the 2017 UEFA European U19
Championship. Named in Gareth
Southgate's 33-man provisional
squad for UEFA Euro 2020,
the Arsenal stopper originally
missed out on making the final
26 but was called up one game
into the tournament after Dean
Henderson withdrew through
injury. He featured in UEFA
Nations League matches against
Italy and Hungary in 2022.

Date/Place of Birth:
19 April 1992 - Soham
England Debut:
6 June 2018 v Costa Rica (H)

First selected for an England
squad in March 2018, Nick
made his Three Lions Debut as
a 65th-minute substitute for
Jack Butland in a 2-0 win over
Costa Rica three months later.
His competitive debut came
against Kosovo in a UEFA Euro
2020 qualifier in November
2019. He set an individual
England goalkeeping record by
going his first 498 minutes at
senior international level without
conceding a goal before shipping
an effort from Jakub Moder in
a 2-1 win over Poland in March
2021.

DEFENDERS

RB/CB

KYLE WALKER

CB

HARRY MAGUIRE

RB/LB

KIERAN TRIPPIER

Date/Place of Birth:
28 May 1990 - Sheffield
England Debut:
12 November 2011 v Spain (H)

Now in his 12th year in the senior England set-up, Kyle had 68 England caps to his name at the time of writing. The Sheffield-born defender was included in the UEFA Euro 2020 Team of the Tournament and was previously included in the Three Lions squad for UEFA Euro 2016 and the 2018 FIFA World Cup. Under the management of Gareth Southgate, Kyle has operated as a centre-back as part of a back three as well as occupying his regular right-back slot.

Date/Place of Birth:
5 March 1993 - Sheffield
England Debut:
8 October 2017 v Lithuania (A)

A goal in England's 10-0 win over San Marino in November 2021 saw Harry become England's top scoring centre-back with seven strikes – one more than ex-Three Lions defender John Terry. The Manchester United defender netted against Sweden in Samara in the 2018 FIFA World Cup quarter-final and also scored in the 4-0 win over Ukraine at UEFA Euro 2020 as he was included in the Team of the Tournament a few weeks later.

Date/Place of Birth:
19 September 1990 - Bury
England Debut:
13 June 2017 v France (A)

Kieran's England career highlights so far include his perfectly executed free-kick to give England the lead in their semi-final clash with Croatia at the 2018 FIFA World Cup. He was ranked as the most creative player at that tournament, having created 24 chances in the six matches in which he featured. On the back of winning the La Liga title with Atletico Madrid in 2020/21, the right-back played in five matches for England at UEFA Euro 2020. He supplied the assist for Luke Shaw to score the Three Lions' opener in the final against Italy.

CB

JOHN STONES

Date/Place of Birth: 28 May 1994 - Barnsley
England Debut: 30 May 2014 v Peru (H)

Previously capped at U19, U20 and U21 level, John was included in England senior squads for UEFA Euro 2016, the 2018 FIFA World Cup and the delayed UEFA Euro 2020. He featured in all seven games at the latter two tournaments. He scored twice in a 6-1 win over Panama in the group stage at the 2018 World Cup and also represented England at the 2019 UEFA Nations League finals. At club level, John is a four-time Premier League winner with Manchester City.

CB

TYRONE MINGS

Date/Place of Birth:
13 March 1993 – Bath
England Debut: 14 October 2019
v Bulgaria (A)

Tyrone featured in England's opening two UEFA Euro 2020 Group D fixtures against Croatia and Scotland, while he came on as a substitute against the Czech Republic at the tournament. The Three Lions won two and drew one of those games, keeping three clean sheets in the process. He scored a stoppage time header in England's 3-0 win over Ivory Coast in March 2022 on the occasion of his 17th senior international appearance.

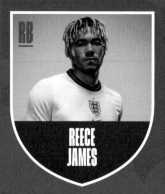

RB

REECE JAMES

Date/Place of Birth:
8 December 1999 – Redbridge
England Debut:
8 October 2020
v Wales (H)

Reece made six appearances prior to UEFA Euro 2020, with the versatile Chelsea player starting his first senior tournament match for the Three Lions against Scotland in the group stage of the competition. Part of the Young Lions squad which won the 2017 UEFA European U19 Championship, Reece started 2022 with ten senior caps to his name, adding to them with UEFA Nations League appearances against Hungary (away), Italy and Hungary (both home).

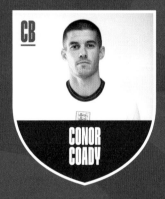

CB

CONOR COADY

RB

TRENT ALEXANDER-ARNOLD

LB

LUKE SHAW

Date/Place of Birth:
25 February 1993 – St Helens
England Debut: 8 September 2020 v Denmark (A)

An unused substitute for England during UEFA Euro 2020, Conor won his tenth senior international cap as he started in the Three Lions' 1-0 away defeat to Hungary in June 2022. Prior to this, Conor represented England at all levels between U16 and U20 and captained the U17s to UEFA European U17 Championship glory back in 2010. A product of Liverpool's youth academy, the defender played at the 2013 FIFA U20 World Cup in Turkey alongside the likes of Harry Kane and John Stones.

Date/Place of Birth:
7 October 1998 – Liverpool
England Debut:
7 June 2018 v Costa Rica (H)

Having missed out on UEFA Euro 2020 through injury, Trent returned to the England fold for the triple-header of 2022 FIFA World Cup qualifying matches in September 2021. The Liverpool right-back started in the 4-0 victory over Andorra that month and also featured in matches in November 2021 and June 2022 to take his caps total to 17. The 2019 Ballon d'Or nominee, who was part of England's 2018 World Cup squad, scored his first international goal in the 3-0 victory over the United States in November 2018.

Date/Place of Birth: 12 July 1995 – Kingston upon Thames
England Debut:
5 March 2014 v Denmark (H)

On the back of scoring for England against Italy in the final of UEFA Euro 2020 – a tournament in which he made three assists in six appearances – he got the Three Lions' first goal of 2022 in a 2-1 friendly win over Switzerland that March. Shaw made his breakthrough into the England senior team whilst playing his club football at Southampton. His Three Lions debut came at his then home ground, St Mary's Stadium, in 2014. He joined Manchester United from Saints later that year.

MIDFIELDERS

JUDE BELLINGHAM

Date/Place of Birth: 23 June 2003 - Stourbridge
England Debut: 12 November 2020 v Republic of Ireland (H)

A product of Birmingham City's academy, Jude became the youngest player to represent the Three Lions at a major tournament when he replaced Harry Kane as an 82nd-minute substitute at the age of 17 years and 349 days in England's opening UEFA Euro 2020 group match against Croatia. The attack-minded midfielder, who was playing his club football for Bundesliga giants Borussia Dortmund at the time of writing, featured in three of England's four UEFA Nations League matches in June 2022.

JORDAN HENDERSON

DECLAN RICE

MASON MOUNT

Date/Place of Birth:
17 June 1990 - Sunderland
England Debut: 17 November 2010 v France (H)

Having failed to score in his first 61 matches for England, Jordan netted twice for the Three Lions in 2021. His strike in the 4-0 win over Ukraine in Rome at the delayed UEFA Euro 2020 was followed by a goal in a 5-0 win over Albania in a World Cup qualifier in November 2021. A two-time England Player of the Year, Jordan had previously represented his country at the 2014 and 2018 FIFA World Cups as well as UEFA Euro 2012 and 2016.

Date/Place of Birth: 14 January 1999 - Kingston upon Thames
England Debut: 22 March 2019 v Czech Republic (H)

Declan featured in all seven of England's matches at UEFA Euro 2020 with 538 minutes on the pitch in total. Since switching his international allegiance from the Republic of Ireland to England in February 2019, the midfielder has made over 30 appearances for the Three Lions with his two international goals at the time of writing having come in a 4-0 triumph over Iceland at Wembley Stadium in November 2020 and in a 4-0 win in Hungary in September 2021.

Date/Place of Birth:
10 January 1999 - Portsmouth
England Debut: 6 September 2019 v Bulgaria (H)

Mason's start against Italy in a UEFA Nations League match in June 2022 saw him become the ninth youngest player to reach the 30 caps mark for England. The Chelsea midfielder was a key figure in the Three Lions' squad at UEFA Euro 2020 as he featured in five tournament matches. A product of Chelsea's youth academy, Mason represented England at various levels between U16 and U21 and was named 'Golden Player' (player of the tournament) at the 2017 UEFA European U19 Championship – a tournament the Young Lions won.

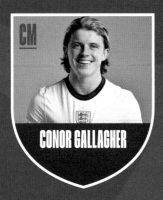

CM

CONOR GALLAGHER

CM

KALVIN PHILLIPS

CM

JAMES WARD-PROWSE

Date/Place of Birth: 6 February 2000 - Epsom
England Debut: 15 November 2021 v San Marino (A)

A season on loan with Crystal Palace during the 2021/22 campaign allowed Chelsea's Conor Gallagher to fully demonstrate his ability, as he scored eight times whilst appearing in 34 of the Eagles' 38 Premier League matches. His form was rewarded with his first senior England call-up in November 2021 while the Surrey-born midfielder collected further caps with appearances against Switzerland and Ivory Coast in March 2022 and Hungary in June 2022.

Date/Place of Birth: 2 December 1995 - Leeds
England Debut: 8 September 2020 v Denmark (A)

When Kalvin made his England debut in September 2020, he became the first Leeds United player since 2004 to represent the Three Lions. A regular in the national team squad ever since, the midfielder's four appearances in four UEFA Nations League matches in June 2022 took his caps tally to 23. He previously featured in all seven matches for the Three Lions at UEFA Euro 2020. In July 2022, Kalvin signed for reigning Premier League champions, Manchester City.

Date/Place of Birth: 1 November 1994 - Portsmouth
England Debut: 22 March 2017 v Germany (A)

An excellent set-piece taker and regular supplier of goals from midfield, James netted for England for the first time in a 5-0 win over San Marino at Wembley Stadium in March 2021. His second goal for the Three Lions, in just his ninth senior international appearance, came in another 5-0 triumph – this time, away in Andorra in October 2021. A product of Southampton's Academy, James previously represented his country between U17 and U21 level.

FORWARDS

FW

HARRY KANE

Date/Place of Birth: 28 July 1993 - London
England Debut: 27 March 2015 v Lithuania (H)

Harry's penalty conversion in the 1-1 UEFA Nations League draw in Germany in June 2022 was his 50th international strike, leaving him four goals short of eclipsing Wayne Rooney's all-time scoring record of 53 for England. The Three Lions captain scored four times at UEFA Euro 2020 as England finished tournament runners-up. He had previously been the top goal scorer in UEFA Euro 2020 qualifying with 12 strikes in eight matches while he won the Golden Boot award at the 2018 FIFA World Cup with six strikes in as many games.

RAHEEM STERLING

Date/Place of Birth: 8 December 1994 - Kingston, Jamaica
England Debut: 14 November 2012 v Sweden (A)

BUKAYO SAKA

Date/Place of Birth: 5 September 2001 - London
England Debut: 8 October 2020 v Wales (H)

Transferred from Manchester City to Chelsea in the summer of 2022, Raheem remains a key member of Gareth Southgate's England squad. His performances at UEFA Euro 2020, in which he scored three goals and made one assist in seven matches, saw him named in the Team of the Tournament. His strike in a 3-0 win over Ivory Coast in March 2022 was his 19th goal in his 74th England appearance. In addition to UEFA Euro 2020, Raheem was included in the Three Lions' squads for the 2014 and 2018 FIFA World Cups and UEFA Euro 2016.

Having previously represented England at every level between U16 and U21, Bukayo made his breakthrough at senior level during the 2020/21 season. Having made Gareth Southgate's 26-man squad for UEFA Euro 2020, he scored his first international goal in a 1-0 triumph over Austria in June 2021 in a friendly at Middlesbrough's Riverside Stadium prior to the tournament getting underway. He was named Man of the Match for his performance against Czech Republic in England's final Group D match – one of four fixtures in which he featured during the competition.

JACK GREALISH

TAMMY ABRAHAM

PHIL FODEN

Date/Place of Birth: 10 September 1995 - Birmingham
England Debut: 8 September 2020 v Denmark (A)

Date/Place of Birth: 2 October 1997 - London
England Debut: 10 November 2017 v Germany (H)

Date/Place of Birth: 28 May 2000 - Stockport
England Debut: 5 September 2020 v Iceland (A)

Jack netted for the Three Lions for the first time in a 5-0 away win in Andorra in October 2021 on the occasion of his 16th international appearance. He made two assists in five UEFA Euro 2020 appearances, setting up Raheem Sterling's winner against Czech Republic and Harry Kane's header against Germany. Previously capped by the Republic of Ireland at U17, U18 and U21 level he switched international allegiance in order to represent the country of his birth at U21 and senior level.

Tammy won his first England caps as the Three Lions hosted Germany and Brazil in friendly matches in November 2017. His first competitive appearance came in a 2-1 away defeat to Czech Republic in October 2019 in a UEFA Euro 2020 qualifier while his first international goal came in a 7-0 victory over Montenegro the following month. The Roma forward has previously been capped at U18, U19 and U21 level.

Aged 20 years and 174 days at the time, Phil's brace in a 4-0 UEFA Nations League victory over Iceland in November 2020 saw him become the youngest England player ever to score two goals at Wembley Stadium. The Manchester City player started in England's 1-0 win over Croatia in their opening match at UEFA Euro 2020 whilst the 2021/22 season saw him named both the Premier League and Professional Footballers' Association Young Player of the Year for the second successive year.

LEAH WILLIAMSON

CAPTAIN

ENGLAND SENIOR

5

FIFA WOMEN'S WORLD CUP APPEARANCES

BEST PERFORMANCE	THIRD PLACE	2015

20 - 0

BT

BIGGEST WIN

20-0 v LATVIA (H)

30 NOVEMBER 2021

TOP SCORER

52 ELLEN WHITE

9 UEFA WOMEN'S EUROPEAN CHAMPIONSHIP APPEARANCES

BEST PERFORMANCE **WINNERS** **2022**

WOMEN'S PROFILE

FIRST INTERNATIONAL
3-2 v SCOTLAND (A)
18 NOVEMBER 1972

MOST CAPS

172
FARA WILLIAMS

SARINA WIEGMAN
HEAD COACH

STAFF PROFILES

SARINA WIEGMAN | MANAGER

Sarina Wiegman led the Lionesses to European Championship glory in the summer of 2022. In doing so, the Dutchwoman achieved something no coach has ever done before - to win back-to-back Euros with two different countries - as she also led the Netherlands to victory on home turf in UEFA Women's Euro 2017.

As a youngster, Wiegman was a standout footballer who earned her first senior Netherlands call-up at just 16 years of age. After a spell playing in the United States for the renowned North Carolina Tar Heels, Wiegman returned to the Netherlands and worked part-time as a PE teacher during her nine-year stay at club side Ter Leede. She retired from playing in 2003 having earned the last of her 104 caps for the Dutch national team. She had become the first Dutch player - male or female - to reach a century of international caps in the process.

Wiegman first ventured into management in 2006, leading her former side Ter Leede to a league and cup double - their first silverware for three years. After a memorable debut season as a manager, she left for ADO Den Haag. She then moved to the Netherlands national team's management staff, where she spent three years as assistant manager first to Roger Reijners and then to Arjan van der Laan, with a short spell as interim manager in between. In October 2016, she simultaneously became assistant manager of the Sparta Rotterdam men's youth team and became the first woman to coach in the professional men's game in Holland.

D.O.B: **26 October 1969**
Place of Birth: **The Hague, Netherlands**
England Women's Manager Since: **September 2021**

Just before Christmas of the same year, she became Netherlands interim boss for the second time as was handed the job on a permanent basis the following month. Wiegman led the Dutch to a stunning title win at UEFA Women's Euro 2017. Her side won every match, including victories over Norway, Sweden and England. She won FIFA Women's Coach of the Year as a result.

In 2019, Wiegman led the Dutch to the World Cup final, although they were beaten by eventual champions the United States. In August 2020, she agreed to become the new Head Coach of the Lionesses following Phil Neville's announcement he would be stepping down in the summer of 2021. She took up the role after coaching the Netherlands women's football team at the delayed Tokyo Olympics in July/August 2021, leading England to UEFA Women's Euro 2022 less than 10 months later!

ARJAN VEURINK ASSISTANT MANAGER

Born in Ommen in the Netherlands on 23 September 1986, Arjan Veurink has had a successful coaching career in women's football. He was appointed Head Coach of Vrouwen Eredivisie FC Twente back in 2012 at the age of just 25. During his four year spell in charge of the Dutch club, the 'Tukkers' won four league titles as well as the KNVB Cup. Twente made it to the knockout phase of the UEFA Women's Champions League in each of his final three seasons with the club.

Prior to his spell in charge at FC Twente, Veurink had served as assistant coach there between 2008 and 2010 while his first managerial role came with the Hengelo-based side ATC '65, for whom he led between 2010 and 2012.

Veurink's success at club level brought him to the attention of the Netherlands women's national team. He became current England women's team Head Coach Sarina Wiegman's assistant when she took charge of the Dutch women's national side in 2017. The pair enjoyed great success with the 'Oranje', as their side won the UEFA Women's European Championships in 2017 and followed that up with an appearance in the final of the 2019 FIFA Women's World Cup.

Following Wiegman's appointment as England's new Head Coach in August 2020, the Royal Dutch Football Association approved her request for Veurink to become her assistant in January 2021. Both agreed to take up their roles with the Football Association in September 2021 after leading the Netherlands at the delayed 2020 Summer Olympics in Tokyo. The Netherlands reached the quarter-finals of that competition, going down to a 4-2 penalty shout-out defeat to the eventual bronze medallist, the United States, after their last-eight tie had finished in a 2-2 draw after extra-time.

Veurink took his place alongside Weigman as she took charge of her first England match against North Macedonia at St Mary's Stadium, Southampton on 17 September 2021.

WOMEN'S SENIOR TEAM

(H) Home (A) Away (N) Neutral Venue   *Information correct as of August 2022

GOALKEEPERS

MARY EARPS

HANNAH HAMPTON

ELLIE ROEBUCK

Date/Place of Birth:
07 March 1993 - Nottingham
England Debut: 11 June 2017 v
Switzerland (A)

Date/Place of Birth:
16 November 2000 - Birmingham
England Debut: 20 February
2022 v Spain (N)

Date/Place of Birth:
23 September 1999 - Sheffield
England Debut:
08 November 2018 v Austria (A)

An ever-present for England at UEFA Women's Euro 2022, Mary kept four clean sheets in six matches en route to the Lionesses' famous triumph. Success is nothing new for the Manchester United goalkeeper, who was part of the same Great Britain squad as Fran Kirby and Demi Stokes that won gold at the 2013 Summer Universiade. Having previously featured for the Lionesses at U17, U19 and U23 level, Mary's appearances at Euro 2022 took her senior cap count to 25.

Hannah was selected for England's Euro 2022 squad after impressing with her form in the 2021/22 Women's Super League (WSL) campaign for Aston Villa. The young goalkeeper had made her senior international debut earlier in the year during England's successful Arnold Clark Cup campaign. With a shut out on her debut, she went on to keep another clean sheet in their emphatic 10-0 win over North Macedonia in a 2023 FIFA Women's World Cup qualifier in April 2022. Hannah has also been capped by England at all levels between U15 and U21.

Ellie was recalled to the England squad in February 2022 for the Arnold Clark Cup where she played in their 3-1 win over Germany, to bring her total number of senior caps to eight. Following a bright start to her international career, the Manchester City shot-stopper missed much of the 2021/22 FA WSL season - and Sarina Wiegman's first few camps as England head coach - with a calf injury. The former Sheffield United's Centre of Excellence attendee was one of three goalkeepers selected for the Lionesses Euro 2022 squad, but didn't feature.

DEFENDERS

RB

LUCY BRONZE

Date/Place of Birth: 28 October 1991 - Berwick-upon-Tweed
England Debut: 26 June 2013 v Japan (H)

One of England Women's most impressive performers for almost a decade, Lucy was just four caps away from making 100 senior appearances for her country at the time of writing. The defender started all six of the Lionesses games at Euro 2022, scoring in the 4-0 semi-final triumph over Sweden. At club level she has won every domestic honour in England, and in France helped Lyon win nine trophies in three seasons including the Champions League. In 2020, Lucy was named BBC Women's Footballer of the Year for a second time and was also crowned The Best FIFA Women's Player, becoming the first English footballer to win the award.

CB

MILLIE BRIGHT

LB

DEMI STOKES

CB

LOTTE WUBBEN-MOY

Date/Place of Birth:
21 August 1993 - Chesterfield
England Debut: 20 September 2016 v Belgium (A)

Millie is one of the most experienced and reliable members of the Lionesses team and started all six games at Euro 2022. Her appearances at the tournament brought her tally of senior England caps to 58, while she has five goals to her name. The Chelsea defender featured in five of England's matches at the 2019 FIFA Women's World Cup while she was included in the Team GB squad for the delayed Tokyo Olympic Games in the summer of 2021.

Date/Place of Birth:
12 December 1991 - Dudley
England Debut: 17 January 2014 v Norway (N)

By the end of Euro 2022, Demi had 67 England caps to her name. Her one and only international goal at the time of writing came in a 9-0 victory over Montenegro in a 2015 FIFA Women's World Cup qualifier in Brighton, a few months after her first senior appearance. The Manchester City player featured for the Lionesses in the 2019 FIFA Women's World Cup – against Japan in the group stage and in their quarter-final win over Norway.

Date/Place of Birth:
11 January 1999 - London
England Debut: 23 February 2021 v Northern Ireland (H)

Lotte made her England senior international debut as a substitute for Arsenal teammate Leah Williamson in a 6-0 victory over Northern Ireland in February 2021. Since then, the defender has made a further seven appearances for the Lionesses and was selected for the Arnold Clark Cup squad in February 2022, but had to withdraw through injury. She captained England U17s at the 2016 FIFA U17 Women's World Cup, leading them to the quarter-finals.

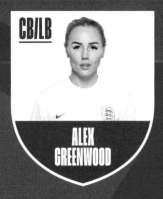

CB/LB

ALEX GREENWOOD

LB

JESS CARTER

RB/FW

RACHEL DALY

Date/Place of Birth:
07 September 1993 - Liverpool
England Debut: 05 March 2014
v Italy (N)

Featuring in five of England's six games on their way to European Championship glory in July 2022, Alex came off the bench at crucial stages in the tournament. She is one of the most experienced Lionesses, having won 66 caps at the time of writing, since breaking into the senior side in 2014. Having previously appeared for England at the 2015 FIFA Women's World Cup, the energetic left-back – who can also play at centre-back - was one of the stars of the 2019 tournament. She has five senior strikes to her name including a brace in the Lionesses 10-0 win over Luxembourg in a 2023 FIFA World Cup qualifier in 2021.

Date/Place of Birth:
27 October 1997 - Warwick
England Debut: 28 November 2017 v Kazakhstan (H)

Jess won her eleventh senior England cap at Euro 2022, when she came off the bench in the Lionesses 5-0 victory over Northern Ireland in the group stage. The Chelsea regular represented England at U19, U20 and U23 level before receiving her first international senior call-up during the qualifying stages for the 2019 FIFA Women's World Cup. Jess' debut followed in the 5-0 win over Kazakhstan in 2017 but it was almost four years later that she was asked to play for the Lionesses again – in September 2021. Her first, and at the time of writing, only goal for England, came in a record-breaking 20-0 victory over Latvia in a 2023 FIFA Women's World Cup qualifier.

Date/Place of Birth:
06 December 1991 - Harrogate
England Debut:
04 June 2016 v Serbia (H)

A key member of Sarina Wiegman's victorious side at Euro 2022, Rachel started all six games in the tournament at left-back. The versatile player – who can operate in defence or attack - now has 57 senior caps at the time of writing, and her strike against Belgium in a friendly in June 2022, took her international goals tally to eight. She plies her trade for National Women's Soccer League (NWSL) side Houston Dash, where she was named their most valuable player in 2018. Rachel was also included in Great Britain's squad for the Tokyo 2020 Olympic Games, featuring in all of the matches.

MIDFIELDERS

CM

KEIRA WALSH

Date/Place of Birth: 08 April 1997 - Rochdale
England Debut: 28 November 2017 v Kazakhstan (H)

Keira's performance in the Euro 2022 final against Germany - which included setting up Ella Toone's opening goal - saw her named Player of the Match. The midfielder started all six games at the tournament and at the time of writing had made 48 senior appearances for the Lionesses altogether. The Manchester City playmaker appeared in all three of England's matches as they won the SheBelieves Cup in 2019 and also helped the Lionesses claim the Arnold Cup in February 2022.

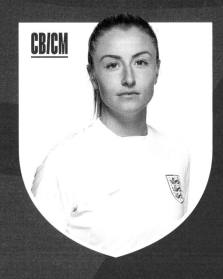

CB/CM

LEAH WILLIAMSON

Date/Place of Birth: 29 March 1997 - Milton Keynes
England Debut: 08 June 2018 v Russia (A)

First handed the England captaincy for a World Cup qualifier against North Macedonia in September 2021, Leah was given the armband permanently in April 2022. Just three months later, she lifted the European Championship trophy for the Lionesses! A commanding presence on the pitch, the Arsenal player had previously turned out for her country in every age group from the U15s to the senior side. As of August 2022, she had scored two goals for the Lionesses - in a friendly against the Czech Republic in 2019 and in a 10-0 victory over Latvia in World Cup qualification in 2021.

CM/FW

GEORGIA STANWAY

CM

ELLA TOONE

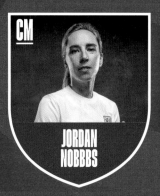

CM

JORDAN NOBBBS

Date/Place of Birth: 03 January 1999 - Barrow-in-Furness
England Debut: 08 November 2018 v Austria (A)

Georgia's stunning extra-time winner against Spain in England's Euro 2022 quarter-final, was her 11th senior international strike. The midfielder played a key role in all six games in the tournament to bring her caps tally to 40. On the back of being named the PFA Women's Young Player of the Year in 2018/19, Georgia was the youngest player to be included in Phil Neville's squad for the 2019 FIFA Women's World Cup, aged 20 at the time. After eight seasons playing for Manchester City, Georgia joined Bundesliga side Bayern Munich in May 2022.

Date/Place of Birth:
2 September 1999 - Tyldesley
England Debut: 23 February 2021 v Northern Ireland (H)

'Super-sub' Ella scored two important goals for the Lionesses on their way to Euro 2022 glory. Her first was an 84th minute equaliser against Spain in the quarter-finals to send the game into extra-time and the midfielder's second came in the Final against Germany, to give England the lead.
The Manchester United regular has now been capped 21 times for the Lionesses, netting 13 goals since making her senior international debut in February 2021 – six of those strikes came from hat-tricks in 2023 FIFA World Cup qualifiers.

Date/Place of Birth:
08 December 1992 - Stockton-on-Tees
England Debut: 06 March 2013 v Italy (N)

Jordan's promise as a young player was emphasised when she was called into the England U15 squad at the age of 12 and captained the side against Wales at 13. Also capped at U17, U19, U20 and U23 level, her senior Lionesses debut came at the age of 19. Having appeared for the Lionesses at the 2013 and 2017 UEFA Women's Championships and the 2015 FIFA Women's World Cup, the Arsenal player suffered the heartbreak of missing out on the 2019 FIFA Women's World Cup and UEFA Women's Euro 2022 with a knee injury.

CM

KATIE ZELEM

Date/Place of Birth: 20 January 1996 - Oldham
England Debut: 23 February 2021 v 30 November 2021 v Latvia (H)

First called into a Lionesses' senior squad for a September 2020 training camp, Katie replaced Keira Walsh as a substitute in England's record 20-0 victory over Latvia in November 2021 to make her senior international debut. Capped between U15 and U23 level, Katie represented England at the FIFA U20 World Cup in Canada in 2014 and helped the U19s to a second-place finish at the U19 EURO Finals the year before that. She comes from a footballing family with both her father Alan and uncle Peter having played the game professionally.

FORWARDS

FW

CHLOE KELLY

CM/FW

FRAN KIRBY

FW

ALESSIA RUSSO

Date/Place of Birth:
15 January 1998 - London
England Debut: 08 November 2018 v Austria (A)

Chloe secured her place in Lionesses immortality, coming off the bench to score the winning goal in the 2-1 extra-time Euro 2022 Final victory over Germany. Her only previous England strike came in a friendly - a 3-0 win over Belgium in the run up to the tournament. Having previously played for Arsenal and Everton, Chloe won the Women's FA Cup in her first year at Manchester City in 2020 and the Women's League Cup, the following campaign. The West Londoner has been a regular in the Lionesses squad since making her senior international debut in 2018.

Date/Place of Birth: 29 June 1993 - Reading
England Debut: 03 August 2014 v Sweden (H)

Fran started in all six games for Sarina Wiegman's team at Euro 2022, scoring memorable goals in the group stage victory over Northern Ireland and the semi-final triumph against Sweden. The midfielder has been capped 63 times for England at senior level at the time of writing, netting 17 strikes since her debut in 2014. At club level, she scored the opening goal of the 2020/21 FA Cup Final for Chelsea to help her team lift the trophy and secure the domestic quadruple – the first English women's club to do so. Fran also won the FWA Women's Footballer of the Year award at the end of that campaign.

Date/Place of Birth:
08 February 1999 - Maidstone
England Debut:
11 March 2020 v Spain (N)

Alessia's audacious back-heel in England's Euro 2022 semi-final victory over Sweden - which earned the striker the 'Goal of the Tournament' award - is one of the abiding memories of a glorious summer for the Lionesses. The strike took the Manchester United player's tally for England to eight goals in just 12 appearances. The former Chelsea and Brighton & Hove Albion forward scored her first England goals with a hat-trick against Latvia during the Lionesses' record 20-0 win in November 2021.

ST

BETHANY ENGLAND

FW

LAUREN HEMP

FW

NIKITA PARRIS

Date/Place of Birth: 03 June 1994 - Barnsley
England Debut: 29 August 2019 v Belgium (A)

Bethany received her first senior call-up for England in their double header against Belgium and Norway in August 2019, following appearances at both U19 and U23 level. The striker's first international goal came in a 2-1 defeat to Brazil in October that year and she was on target again a month later against the Czech Republic. Bethany has made 19 senior appearances, netting nine goals at the time of writing – the most recent being in a friendly against Switzerland in June 2022. The Chelsea player – who has won numerous trophies at club level - was selected for the Lionesses' Euro 2022 squad, but didn't feature at the tournament.

Date/Place of Birth: 07 August 2000 - North Walsham
England Debut: 08 October 2019 v Portugal (A)

A four-time PFA Women's Young Player of the Year, Lauren already had 28 England senior caps and eight goals to her name by the time she celebrated her 22nd birthday in August 2022. The striker started every game as the Lionesses triumphed at the European Championships, scoring once in the 8-0 thumping of Norway in the group stage. Back in 2018, she helped the Young Lionesses finish third at that year's FIFA U20 Women's World Cup. She has won both the FA Women's Cup and Women's League Cup with her FA WSL side, Manchester City, since joining the Citizens in 2018.

Date/Place of Birth:
10 March 1994 - Toxteth
England Debut: 04 June 2016 v Serbia (H)

Nikita featured in two games as the Lionesses triumphed at Euro 2022, to bring her international caps tally to 67. The striker has scored important goals during her England career. She slotted home a penalty in the 2-1 win over Scotland in the 2019 FIFA Women's World Cup opening Group D fixture in Nice, got the winner against Portugal at UEFA Women's Euro 2017 and was also on target against the United States in the successful 2019 SheBelieves Cup campaign. In August 2022, Nikita signed for FA WSL side Manchester United from Arsenal.

FW

BETH MEAD

Date/Place of Birth: 09 May 1995 - Whitby
England Debut: 06 April 2018 v Wales (H)
Beth picked up the 'Golden Boot' award at Women's Euro 2022 with six goals en route to winning the tournament with the Lionesses. Those strikes included the only goal against Austria in a 1-0 victory and her fourth career hat-trick against Norway in the group phase. The Arsenal forward was also part of the squad who lifted the Arnold Clark Cup in February 2022. With 28 goals from 45 senior international appearances at the time of writing, Beth is an integral member of Sarina Wiegman's squad.

MEN'S SENIOR MATCHES 2022

Gareth Southgate's side prepared for their appearance at the FIFA World Cup with a series of friendlies and UEFA Nations League matches in 2022.

ENGLAND 2-1 SWITZERLAND **FRIENDLY**

26 MARCH 2022
WEMBLEY STADIUM. LONDON

ENGLAND: Pickford, Walker-Peters (Sterling 62), Guehi, Coady, White, Shaw (Mitchell 61), Gallagher (Rice 61), Henderson, Mount (Grealish 62), Foden (Bellingham 80), Kane (Watkins 89)

SWITZERLAND: Omlin, Widmer (Mbabuat 36), Akanji, Frei, Embolo (Gavranovic 80), Freuler (Zuber 63), Xhaka, Steffen (Zeqiri 62), Rodriguez, Vargas (Sow 63), Shaqiri (Aebischer 80)

After previously scoring in the UEFA Euro 2020 Final, Luke Shaw bagged his second-ever England goal in an entertaining friendly victory over Switzerland.

The Three Lions fell behind after 22 minutes of the encounter to a Breel Embolo header. Shaw's leveller came in first-half stoppage time, after England debutant Kyle Walker-Peters charged down an attempted clearance from Swiss midfielder Fabian Frei allowing Conor Gallagher to play the ball into his path to score.

On an occasion in which Marc Guehi and Tyrick Mitchell also made their senior international debuts, England were grateful to the contribution of goalkeeper Jordan Pickford, who made a number of excellent saves during the match. The Three Lions' winner came 12 minutes from time after substitute Steven Zuber was adjudged to have handled in his own penalty area. Skipper Harry Kane scored the resulting spot-kick as he drew level with Sir Bobby Charlton as England's second-top goal scorer of all time with 49 goals.

ENGLAND   COTE D'IVOIRE FRIENDLY

ENGLAND: Pope, White (Walker-Peters 45), Maguire, Mings, Mitchell (Shaw 62), Ward-Prowse (Gallagher 80), Rice, Bellingham, Grealish (Smith Rowe 62), Watkins (Kane 62), Sterling (Foden 62)

COTE D'IVOIRE: Ali, Kamara, Deli, Bailly (Agbadou 45), Aurier, Seri (Akouokou 90+3), Kessie, Gradel (Coulibaly 45), Cornet (Konan 64), Pepe (Boly 45), Haller (Boli 86)

Raheem Sterling scored and made an assist in a comfortable friendly win for England against Ivory Coast.

The Manchester City forward bamboozled his marker before sliding an exquisite pass across the Ivory Coast six-yard-box, which Ollie Watkins was able to tap home from close range. Ivorian defender Serge Aurier was sent-off for a second bookable offence on 40 minutes before Sterling doubled England's advantage on the stroke of half-time, as he scored from a Jack Grealish assist.

VAR overturned the awarding of an England penalty early in the second half but in stoppage time at the end of the match, the Three Lions got their third goal of the evening as Tyrone Mings headed in from a Phil Foden corner.

HUNGARY 1-0 ENGLAND UEFA NATIONS LEAGUE
4 JUNE 2022
PUSKAS ARENA, BUDAPEST

HUNGARY: Gulácsi, Lang, Orbán, Attila Szalai, Négo, Ádám Nagy (Styles 82), Schäfer, Zsolt Nagy (Vécsei 87), Sallai (Kleinheisler 71), Szoboszlai (Fiola 82), Ádám Szalai (Ádám 87)

ENGLAND: Pickford, Walker (Stones 62), Coady (Phillips 79), Maguire, Alexander-Arnold (James 62), Bellingham, Rice, Justin (Saka 46), Bowen, Kane, Mount (Grealish 62)

Jarrod Bowen and James Justin both made their senior England debuts as the Three Lions' UEFA Nations League Group A3 campaign got underway in Budapest.

The decisive moment of the match came just after the hour mark when Reece James was adjudged to have tripped Zsolt Nagy in the England penalty area. Dominik Szoboszlai converted the resulting spot-kick, which was enough for a Hungary win in the end. It was the Three Lions' first defeat, other than losing to Italy on penalties in the UEFA Euro 2020 final, since Belgium beat them in November 2020.

GERMANY | ENGLAND UEFA NATIONS LEAGUE
7 JUNE 2022
FUSBALL ARENA MUNCHEN, MUNICH

GERMANY: Neuer, Schlotterbeck, Rüdiger, Klostermann, J Hofmann (Gnabry 65), Gündoğan (Sané 84), Kimmich, Raum, Müller (Goretzka 75), Musiala (Werner 66), Havertz

ENGLAND: Pickford, Walker, Stones, Maguire, Trippier, Rice, Phillips (Bellingham 15), Saka (Bowen 80), Mount (Grealish 72), Sterling, Kane

Harry Kane's late penalty against Germany, which gave the Three Lions a UEFA Nations League point, saw him become just the second England senior men's player to score 50 goals for his country.

Kane was awarded the penalty, which he converted with two minutes left of the 90, after a VAR review ruled he had been brought down by Nico Schlotterbeck. He sent German goalkeeper Manuel Neuer the wrong way with his kick.

Germany had taken a 50th-minute lead in the match when Jonas Hofmann's powerful shot went in, despite Jordan Pickford getting a strong hand to the ball. There was no shortage of chances for either side to win the game, with six shots on target for each side over the course of the match.

ENGLAND 0-0 ITALY

ENGLAND: Ramsdale, James, Maguire, Tomori (Guéhi 88), Trippier; Rice (Phillips 65), Ward-Prowse, Sterling (Saka 79), Mount (Bowen 66), Grealish, Abraham (Kane 65)

ITALY: Donnarumma, Di Lorenzo, Gatti, Acerbi, Dimarco (Florenzi 88), Frattesi, Locatelli (Gnonto 65), Tonali, Pessina (Cristante 88), Scamacca (Raspadori 77), Pellegrini (Esposito 65)

England picked up their second point of the UEFA Nations League campaign after a goalless draw with reigning European champions, Italy.

Both teams had good opportunities to get the win. Mason Mount thrashed a right-footed shot against the crossbar after nine minutes of the match while Declan Rice's shot from a James Ward-Prowse corner narrowly missed the target. At the other end, Aaron Ramsdale made two excellent saves from Sandro Tonali and Matteo Pessina.

Arguably the best chance of the match fell to England's captain on the night, Raheem Sterling, who was unable to keep his shot down from a wonderful Reece James cross early in the second half.

ENGLAND 0-4 HUNGARY

ENGLAND: Ramsdale, James, Guéhi, Stones, Walker; Gallagher (Mount 56), Phillips, Bellingham (Foden 68), Saka (Maguire 85), Kane, Bowen (Sterling 46)

HUNGARY: Dibusz, Lang, Orbán, At. Szalai, Fiola, Schäfer, Styles (A Nagy 55), Z Nagy, Szoboszlai (Gazdag 55), Sallai (Négo 78), Ad. Szalai (Ádám 68)

It was a night to forget for England in Wolverhampton against a rampant Hungary. A brace from Roland Sallai and further goals from Zsolt Hagy and Daniel Gazdag condemned the Three Lions to their worst home defeat since 1928.

John Stones was sent-off for a second bookable offence on 82 minutes, compounding a disappointing evening for Gareth Southgate's men. England's Group A3 campaign concluded in September 2022 with an away game against Italy and a home clash with Germany at Wembley Stadium.

THAT WAS THEN

30 November 2022 marked the 150th anniversary of the world's first international association football match between Scotland and England.

Between 1870 and 1872, a series of five friendly matches were played between teams representing England and Scotland. The first game, played at The Oval on 5 March 1870 ended in a 1-1 draw, as did a clash on 25 February 1871, while England were 1-0 winners in matches on 19 November 1870 and 24 February 1872 and won 2-1 on 18 November 1871. These matches are not recognised by FIFA – world football's governing body – as full internationals due to the fact Scotland's team for the fixtures comprised only of London-based Scots.

In October 1872, Queen's Park – Scotland's leading club of the time - took up the challenge from then-Football Association Secretary Charles Alcock of putting together a Scottish team to face England in Glasgow. Scotland had hoped to call on the services of The Wanderers' Arthur Kinnaird and Henry Renny-Tailyour of Royal Engineers but both were unavailable. So, all eleven Scottish players came from Queen's Park. England meanwhile called upon three players from Oxford University while the rest came from Cambridge University, Hertfordshire Rangers, Notts County, 1st Surrey Rifles, Sheffield Wednesday, Crystal Palace and Barnes. Alcock himself was unable to play due to injury.

The match was arranged for St Andrew's Day (30 November) 1872 at the West of Scotland Cricket Club's Hamilton Crescent ground in the Partick area of Glasgow. Initially scheduled for a 2pm kick-off, the start of the game was delayed by 20 minutes as some 4,000 spectators packed into the ground. Both teams wore the traditional colours associated

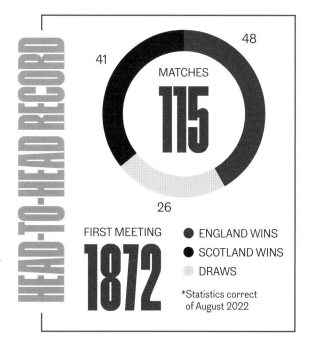

INTERNATIONAL FOOT-BALL MATCH, (ASSOCIATION RULES,)

ENGLAND v. SCOTLAND,

WEST OF SCOTLAND CRICKET GROUND,

HAMILTON CRESCENT, PARTICK,

SATURDAY, 30th November, 1872, at 2 p.m.

ADMISSION—ONE SHILLING.

HEAD-TO-HEAD RECORD

41

48

MATCHES

115

26

FIRST MEETING

1872

- ● ENGLAND WINS
- ● SCOTLAND WINS
- ○ DRAWS

*Statistics correct of August 2022

with them today – Scotland in dark blue shirts while England wore white shirts with the distinctive Three Lions on their left breast and wore caps while the Scots wore red cowls.

Contemporary reports generally acknowledge that Scotland - benefitting from their players coming from the same club side – performed best in the first half of the encounter while England more than matched them in the second. Interestingly, both sides rotated goalkeeping duties at half-time with William Maynard replacing Robert Barker between the sticks during the interval while Scottish captain Robert Gardner handed over responsibilities to Robert Smith.

THE WORLD'S FIRST INTERNATIONAL MATCH

30 November 1872
SCOTLAND 0-0 ENGLAND
Hamilton Crescent, Glasgow

SCOTLAND (With club side listed)

Robert Gardner (C) - Queens Park
William Ker - Queens Park
Joseph Taylor - Queens Park
James J. Thomson - Queens Park
James Smith - Queens Park
Robert Smith - Queens Park
Robert Leckie - Queens Park
Alex Rhind - Queens Park
Billy MacKinnon - Queens Park
Jerry Weir - Queens Park
David Wotherspoon - Queens Park

Scotland had a 'goal' disallowed early in the second half when the umpires decided the shot had cleared the tape used to represent the cross bar. A late Robert Leckie shot nestled on top of the tape meanwhile.

Despite the match finishing in a goalless draw, the fixture which came to be recognised by FIFA as the world's first international match drew widespread praise.

"It was allowed to be the best game ever seen in Scotland", wrote the Aberdeen Journal while sport magazine The Field commented that, "The result was received with rapturous applause by the spectators and the cheers proposed by each XI for their antagonists were continued by the onlookers until the last member of the two sides had disappeared."

ENGLAND (With club sides listed)

Robert Barker - Hertfordshire Rangers
Harwood Greenhalgh – Notts County
Reginald Courtenay Welch – Harrow Chequers
Frederick Maddison – Oxford University
William Maynard – 1st Surrey Rifles
John Brockbank – Cambridge University
Charles Clegg – Sheffield Wednesday
Arnold Kirke Smith – Oxford University
Cuthbert Ottaway (C) – Oxford University
Charles Chenery – Crystal Palace
Charles Morice - Barnes

Attendance: 4,000

50 YEARS OF THE LIONESSES

2022 saw England Women host the UEFA Women's European Championships and celebrate their 50th anniversary as a team.

The success of winning the 1966 FIFA World Cup on home soil inspired even greater interest in football across the nation. Three years after this seminal moment, a governing body for women's football was established in England – the Women's Football Association (WFA).

The WFA was responsible for setting up seven regional leagues across England and in 1971, established the forerunner of the FA Women's Cup – the Mitre Trophy. The following year saw the creation of the first England women's team, who beat Scotland 3-2 in Greenock on 18 November 1972. Sylvia Gore holds the distinction of scoring the first-ever goal for England Women at Ravenscraig Stadium. Strikes from Mary Carr and Rose Reilly thereafter put the Scots ahead but a brace from Pat Davies secured England's victory in their inaugural match.

Previously managed by Eric Worthington and Tom Tranter, Martin Reagan took on the top job with the Lionesses in 1979 – a role he would hold through until 1991. During that time, England reached the final of the inaugural 'European Competition for Women's Football' (now UEFA

Women's European Championships) with a 3-1 aggregate victory over Denmark in April 1984. The following month, the Lionesses were beaten 4-3 on penalties by Sweden in the final after a 1-1 aggregate draw.

England once again qualified for the four-team European Competition for Women's Football tournament under Reagan's management once again in 1987. On that occasion, they were beaten 3-2 after extra-time in the semi-finals by Sweden at the Melløs Stadion in Moss, Norway. Reagan's 12-year tenure came to an end after England's quarter-final loss to Germany at the UEFA Women's European Championships in 1991, which left the Lionesses unable to qualify for the inaugural FIFA Women's World Cup. Barrie Williams and then John Bilton took charge of the side thereafter.

In 1993, The Football Association took over the running of the women's game in England. Two years later, the Lionesses qualified for the UEFA Women's European Championships, having missed out on the previous three editions. They also achieved a historic first qualification to the 1995 FIFA Women's World Cup as a result of making it to the semi-finals of the European Championships earlier in the year.

Replacing Ted Copeland in June 1998, Hope Powell became England's first, full-time Head Coach in June 1998. During her 15-year reign, Powell guided the Lionesses to the 2001, 2005, 2009 and 2013 editions of the UEFA Women's Championship and the FIFA Women's World Cup in 2007 and 2011. England's biggest achievement under Powell's management was making it to the Final of the European Championships in 2009.

Powell left the role in August 2013. Many of the Lionesses' current key senior players had forged their way into the England set-up before that time with the likes of Steph Houghton, Jill Scott and Ellen White also included in Great Britain's squad for the 2012 Olympic Games.

England's best showing at a FIFA Women's World Cup to date came in 2015 as the Lionesses finished third at the tournament. Mark Sampson's side won two of their three Group F fixtures to progress to the knockout phase. Victories over Norway and Canada took England to the semi-finals, where they were beaten 2-1 by Japan. A 1-0 extra-time win over Germany saw Sampson's team came out on top in the third-place play-off.

Four years later, with Phil Neville installed as England Head Coach, the Lionesses once again made it to the semi-final of the FIFA Women's World Cup. A 2-1 defeat to the United States in the semi-finals was followed by a 2-1 loss to Sweden in the third-place play-off eventually saw them finish fourth. Later that year, the Lionesses welcomed a record crowd for a home international as 77,768 fans saw them take on Germany at Wembley Stadium.

In the run-up to hosting UEFA Women's Euro 2022, England were in fine form with 2023 FIFA Women's World Cup qualifying results including three, 10-0 away wins in Luxembourg, Latvia and North Macedonia. The Lionesses achieved their record victory with a 20-0 win over Latvia in Doncaster on 30 November 2021 as they ended the year with six wins out of six, 53 goals scored and none conceded!

Coverage of England's success at UEFA Women's Euro 2022 can be found on pages 6-11.

WORDSEARCH

Find the surnames of eight different managers who have been in charge of either the Three Lions or Lionesses.

T	X	J	F	I	R	C	C	J	V	S
Y	C	N	R	A	M	S	E	Y	O	O
N	Z	P	X	R	R	L	G	V	U	
S	E	U	O	G	W	M	P	R	T	
R	A	V	R	W	S	L	T	E	H	
O	N	M	I	U	E	S	A	A	G	
B	A	T	P	L	J	L	Y	G	A	
S	R	D	Q	S	L	H	L	A	T	
O	K	S	I	R	O	E	O	N	E	
N	H	J	W	T	E	N	R	E	L	

Answers on pages 60-61.

NEVILLE   REAGAN   SOUTHGATE
POWELL   ROBSON   TAYLOR
RAMSEY   SAMPSON

QUIZ

TEST YOUR ENGLAND KNOWLEDGE WITH 30 QUESTIONS ON THE THREE LIONS AND LIONESSES.

1. In which Scottish city did England compete in the first FIFA-recognised international football match in November 1872?

2. Who was the first person to captain England Men's team?

3. Who was the first player to score for England Women's team?

4. Who was England Women's Head Coach when the Lionesses were finalists at UEFA Women's Euro 2009?

5. Who were England Women's opponents when they achieved their record win (20-0) in November 2021?

6. With which two clubs did England Head Coach Gareth Southgate win the Football League Cup during his playing career?

7. How many steps did a team captain need to climb to collect a trophy from the Royal Box at the 'original' Wembley Stadium?

8. What year did the current Wembley Stadium open?

9. Who were England's opponents when a record Lionesses' home crowd of 77,768 watched them at Wembley Stadium in 2019?

10. Who did England play in the final of the delayed UEFA Euro 2020?

11. England's UEFA Nations League match against Italy in September 2022 marked how many matches as Three Lions manager for Gareth Southgate?

 A) 50   B) 75   C) 100

12. Which West Ham United coach returned to England's coaching set-up in August 2021?

13. Who is Head Coach of England's Senior Women's team?

14. Who surpassed Kelly Smith's current record of 46 strikes to become England Women's top, all-time goal scorer in December 2021?

15. Who did England face in their first match at UEFA Women's Euro 2022?

16. Who did England face in their first match at the 2022 FIFA World Cup?

17. Which 'home nation' were in Group B along with England at the 2022 FIFA World Cup?

18. Which stadium staged England's Group A match against Northern Ireland at UEFA Women's Euro 2022?

19. With 125 caps, which former goalkeeper is England Men's most capped player?

20. With 172 caps, which former midfielder is England Womens's most capped player?

21. What high-profile club fixture was staged at Wembley Stadium in 2011 and 2013?

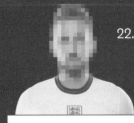

22. Who was England's top-scorer at UEFA Euro 2020 with four strikes?

23. How many goals did England's Cerebral Palsy team score at the 2022 IFCPF World Cup?

A) 5   B) 10   C) 21

24. Which England senior men's team defender made his 50th England appearance against Belgium in October 2020?

25. Against which 'home nation' did Jill Scott make her 150th England appearance in February 2021?

26. Which England goalkeeper achieved a tournament-best five clean sheets at UEFA Euro 2020?

27. Which Spanish club did Lucy Bronze sign for in the summer of 2022?

28. In which South Yorkshire city was Ellie Roebuck born on 23 September 1999?

29. Which former Manchester United player (who scored 49 goals for the Three Lions) did Harry Kane overtake on England's all-time, goal scoring list when he scored his 50th international goal against Germany in June 2022?

30. Along with Marc Guehi and Tyrick Mitchell, which former Tottenham Hotspur defender made his England debut against Switzerland in March 2022?

Answers on pages 60-61.

YOUTH AND DEVELOPMENT TEAM UPDATE

A LOOK BACK ON THE YEAR THAT WAS FOR VARIOUS ENGLAND YOUTH AND DEVELOPMENT TEAMS IN 2022.

WOMEN'S U23s

After back-to-back fixtures against their French counterparts in February, Mo Marley's Women's U23s side travelled to San Pedro del Pinatar in Murcia, Spain for two matches against the Netherlands in April. A goalless draw was followed a few days later by a 3-0 win for England, featuring a brace from Rinsola Babajide, while Marit Auee put through her own net.

WOMEN'S U19s

Gemma Davies' U19s were one of eight teams who competed in the 2022 UEFA Women's U19 Championship in the Czech Republic. The Young Lionesses got off to the perfect start in the tournament with a 4-1 victory over Norway in Karviná. Aggie Beever-Jones scored twice in the win while Jorja Fox and Grace Clinton were also on target. A 1-0 defeat to Sweden and a 3-0 loss to Germany followed as England were eliminated at the group stage. Spain went on to beat Norway 2-1 in the Final.

MEN'S U21s

Lee Carsley's U21s side secured qualification for the 2023 UEFA European U21 Championship by finishing top of their qualifying group, with eight wins, one draw and just one loss in 10 matches.

Having won three and drawn one of their opening four qualifying fixtures in 2021, the Young Lions carried on their good form in 2022. AFC Bournemouth's Vitality Stadium hosted their 4-1 qualifying win over Andorra in March which featured goals from Folarin Balogun, Jacob Ramsey, Morgan Gibbs-White and Anthony Gordon. Balogun bagged a brace as England visited Albania a few days later, with Curtis Jones also registering in the 3-0 win.

Emile Smith Rowe and Ramsey scored in the U21s' 2-1 win in their top-of-the-table clash with the Czech Republic in České Budějovice in June. Four days later, Carsley's team sealed their ninth straight

appearance at the European U21 Championship finals with a 3-0 win over Albania in Chesterfield. Balogun continued his excellent scoring run with two goals while Cameron Archer was also on target. Archer scored twice in the Young Lions' last away match in the qualifying group, as they won 5-0 in Kosovo. Also on target that day were Keane Lewis-Potter and Gordon, while Ilir Krasniqi scored an own-goal. The campaign ended with a 2-1 defeat to Slovenia at Huddersfield Town's John Smith's Stadium – a game in which Archer netted a stoppage time consolation for England.

MEN'S U20s

The 2021/22 season saw England U20s compete in the fourth edition of the U20 Elite League. Andy Edwards' side bounced back from the disappointment of a 2-0 away defeat to Poland in the competition in March to beat Germany 3-1 at Colchester United's JobServe Community Stadium four days later, thanks to goals from Sam Greenwood, James McAtee and Tyrhys Dolan as the tournament continued.

MEN'S U19s

It was a year to remember for England's U19s, who won the UEFA U19 Championship for a second time – having also triumphed in 2017. Ian Foster's team boasted a perfect record in the group stage of the tournament in Slovakia with three wins from three and no goals conceded. First up was a 2-0 triumph over Austria with goals from Carney Chukwuemeka and Alfie Devine. Chukwuemeka was also on target in the 4-0 victory against Serbia, that also featured a Dane Scarlett brace and a further strike from Daniel Jebbison. Liam Delap got the winner in a 1-0 success against Israel in the final group game.

Despite falling behind to a 12th-minute penalty from Fabio Miretti, England scored twice in the second half of their last-four match against Italy to book a place in the Final. Alex Scott and Jarell Quansah got the Young Lions' goals. In the Final against Israel, England fell behind again, as Oscar Gluh scored five minutes from the break. Callum Doyle's second half leveller eventually forced extra-time when Aston Villa duo Chukwuemeka and Aaron Ramsey scored to bring the trophy home for the Young Lions.

MEN'S U18s

There was success for Ryan Garry's U18 side, who won a four-team tournament in Croatia in June 2022. Midfielder Oliver Arblaster came off the bench to score the winner in a 3-2 victory over Austria in the Young Lions' tournament opener. George Hall and Divin Mubama had scored either side of half-time for the Young Lions. Goals from Jude Soonsup-Bell and Sonny Perkins made it two wins from two against Wales while a goalless draw with Croatia meant England won the four nations tournament in Zagreb.

MEN'S U17s

Defeats to Luxembourg and eventual tournament winners, France, in March 2022 denied England's U17s the opportunity to compete at that year's UEFA European U17 Championship. Friendly victories for Tom Curtis' team during 2022 included a 3-0 triumph over Scotland in February – a game in which Tudor Mendel-Idowu bagged a brace, while Leo Castledine was also on target. The Young Lions beat Norway 3-0 during a trip to Marbella in June with goals from Kami Doyle, Victor Akinwale and Jack Griffiths.

GOALS GALORE

England Cerebral Palsy team scored 21 goals in six matches at the 2022 IFCPF World Cup in Barcelona, as they finished sixth at the 16-nation tournament.

England Cerebral Palsy team made an incredible start to the 2022 International Federation of Cerebral Palsy Football (IFCPF) World Cup as they defeated Canada 8-1 in their opening Group A fixture on 3 May 2022. A hat-trick from David Porcher, a brace by Liam Irons and goals from Harry Baker, Matthew Robinson and James Blackwell saw Andy Smith's side complete a convincing victory.

England went one better, beating Venezuela 9-0 in their second fixture two days later. Porcher added to his hat-trick against Canada with five goals against Venezuela – four of which arrived in the opening nine minutes. Baker and Irons were also on target while Sam Dewhirst bagged a brace in the game.

Qualification for the quarter-finals was secured as England drew 1-1 with the Netherlands in their final Group A fixture. A Matt Crossen goal 15 minutes from time (each IFCPF World Cup match lasts 60 minutes) gave the Three Lions an all-important point and they topped their group.

A 3-1 defeat to Iran on 9 May 2022 ended England's hopes of winning the trophy. Dewhirst got the Three Lions' consolation with his third goal at that point of the tournament. Smith's team entered the round robin thereafter to determine their final position at the competition.

A memorable 2-1 win over Argentina ensured the Three Lions would either finish fifth or sixth. Matiaz Fernandez gave the Argentinians a 26th-minute, before Porcher levelled in first-half stoppage time. The winner came in the last minute of the 60 as Crossen converted.

England met the Netherlands once again in the fight for fifth. As per the early group game, the clash on 15 May 2022 finished in a draw after 60 minutes. This time around, no goals were scored and the match went to extra-time and then penalties. Long-serving England goalkeeper Giles Moore made an excellent save from the Dutch's third penalty taker but the Netherland's triumphed 3-2 on spot-kicks as the Three Lions ended sixth at the tournament.

1.

I was born in Jamaica and raised in London, where I attended Copland School in Wembley. I made my England senior debut against Sweden in 2012. I was England's second-highest goal scorer at UEFA Euro 2020 with three strikes.

2.

I am a lifelong Arsenal supporter. I captained the Lionesses for the first time against North Macedonia in September 2021. I was appointed as permanent England captain in April 2022.

WHO AM I?

5.

I am a goalkeeper. I was included in the Lionnesses' squad for the UEFA Women's Euro 2022 and I was allocated the number one shirt for the tournament. I made my senior England debut against Switzerland in June 2017.

6.

I returned to Manchester City from Olympique Lyonnais in 2020, having previously turned out for the Citizens between 2014 and 2017. In 2019, I became the first Lioness to be named in the top three nominees for the Ballon d'Or Féminin.

3.

I am a defender. Having previous played for Everton, Liverpool and Manchester United, I joined Manchester City from Olympique Lyonnais in 2020. I scored for England against Cameroon at the 2019 FIFA Women's World Cup.

4.

I made my senior England debut on at my then-home club ground, St Mary's. I made three assists in six appearances at UEFA Euro 2020. I scored the opening goal in the final of that competition.

Guess the identity of these England players from the following clues...

Answers on pages 60-61.

7.

I played in all seven of England's matches at UEFA Euro 2020. I previously played international football for the Republic of Ireland before switching my international allegiance to England in February 2019. I share my surname with a type of food.

8.

I scored on my senior England debut against Lithuania in March 2015. I won the Golden Boot at the 2018 FIFA World Cup, scoring six goals in as many matches. I was England's top goalscorer at UEFA Euro 2020 with four strikes.

THREE LIONS

From their first international in 1872 to date, England have worn a crest with Three Lions on it. But do you know why? Here, we trace the history of this world-famous emblem.

The crest that was worn by England on the left-breast of their shirt when they took on Scotland in Glasgow in the world's first international match [check out pages 36-37 to read more about the clash] in 1872 bore a close resemblance to the Royal Arms of England. Featuring three rampant, navy blue lions set within a shield, the original crest used on England's shirt back then also incorporated a red and navy crown sat on top.

Like England's shirt, there have been many alterations to the crest over the years but the basic design used by The Football Association has endured for over 150 years...

Royal emblems depicting lions are understood to have been used as far back as the 5th century by Danish Vikings and Germanic Saxons. William the Conqueror (c.1028 – 9 September 1087) used two lions on a red background as his coat of arms and brought this symbol to the English throne when he ruled as King of England between 25 December 1066 and 9 September 1087. Richard I – AKA Richard the Lionheart –

used a single lion as an armorial seal between 1189 and 1198. King Henry II, who ruled from 19 December 1154 to 6 July 1189, added a lion to William the Conqueror's two when he married Eleanor of Aquitaine in 1152, with this personal coat of arms becoming the Royal Arms of England when he came to the throne two years later.

The Royal Arms of England have featured Three Lions ever since and were incorporated into the Royal Coat of Arms of the United Kingdom, which was adopted in 1873, appearing in the first and fourth quarters. It is an unofficial symbol for the nation of England 1963 to celebrate The Football Association's centenary with the words 'CENTENARY YEAR 1863-1963' emblazoned above and below the crest. On 9 January 1979, The Football Association received a second grant of arms, which expanded the crest to a emblem was used on the white shorts launched in 2009, while an all-red logo was introduced on shirts launched in 2012 and 2020 shirt, while there was an all-white crest on the 2012/13 away shirt. The full colour crest has once again featured on the most recent

ON A SHIRT

and has been adopted by many English sporting bodies such as the England and Wales Cricket Board (ECB), England Hockey and England Boxing to be used as an official crest and on their team equipment/kit.

On 30 March 1949, The Football Association was granted a coat of arms which saw some variation to the original crest introduced. In addition to the three blue lions, ten red Tudor roses were added to the design, each representing one of the ten regional divisions who had a seat of the Football Association Council. This was updated a year later to include an eleventh Tudor rose.

A commemorate emblem was used during the calendar year of

full heraldic achievement, which included a peregrine falcon, the motto 'Play The Game' on a scroll and two additional lions in blue and white, holding the shield of the Three Lions. There is no evidence this crest was ever used and both The Football Association and the England national team continued to be represented by the traditional Three Lions crest, pretty much as it appears today.

The colour and design of the logo has had many subtle changes over the years, not least the colour blue used on the lions, which has appeared in many shades from dark navy blue to sky blue. From 2009 to date, a series of single-colour crests England's various kit elements – an all-white

England kits.

No review of the history of England's famous crest would be complete without a mention of the song inspired by it - 'Three Lions' (Football's Coming Home). Co-written by David Baddiel, Frank Skinner and Ian Broudie and performed with the Lightning Seeds, Three Lions was produced ahead of UEFA Euro 1996. The song reached number one in the UK Singles chart in both 1996 and again in 2018, on the back of England's run to the semi-finals of that summer's FIFA World Cup. The re-worded '3 Lions '98' reached number one in the UK singles chart during England's appearance at the 1998 FIFA World Cup in France.

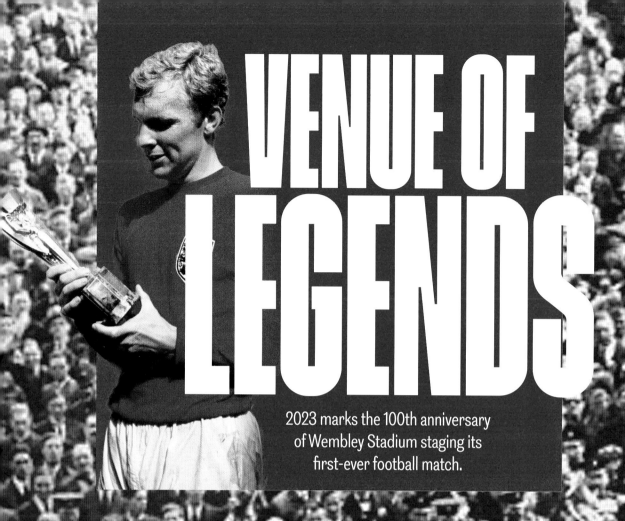

VENUE OF LEGENDS

2023 marks the 100th anniversary of Wembley Stadium staging its first-ever football match.

The 'original' Wembley Stadium, with its distinctive twin towers, was built in 300 days between 1922 and 1923. The venue opened in April 1923, staging that year's FA Cup Final. It continued to host FA Cup Finals, League Cup finals, the 1966 FIFA World Cup, UEFA Euro 1996 and five European Cup finals - and was also home to the England national team - through until its closure in October 2000 and subsequent demolition.

The so-called 'Home of Football' also hosted many other events including American football, rugby league, rugby union, greyhound racing, speedway, concerts and the 1948 Summer Olympics. It was replaced by the current Wembley Stadium, which opened in 2007 and continues to host England international matches, the FA Cup Final and other top-class sporting and non-sporting events.

THE EARLY YEARS

Wembley's largest-ever attendance of 126,047 packed into the ground for the venue's first match – the FA Cup Final between Bolton Wanderers and West Ham United on 28 April 1923. The actual number of fans inside the stadium for Wanderers' 2-0 victory is understood to have far exceeded the official attendance figure with estimates that between 200,000 and 300,000 people gained admission that afternoon. The crowd overflowed onto the pitch and it took a number of mounted police – most famously Police Constable George Scorey and his white horse, Billy, to clear the playing surface. The match was later dubbed the 'White Horse Final' as result.

After that match, every subsequent FA Cup Final at Wembley Stadium – bar the 1982 replay – was made all-ticket to avoid overcrowding.

Wembley Stadium was the centrepiece of the 1924/25 British Empire Stadium and was originally known as the 'British Empire Exhibition Stadium'

or more commonly, the 'Empire Stadium'. Designed by Sir John Simpson and Maxwell Ayrton and built by Sir Robert McAlpine at a cost of £750,000 (equivalent to around £50m in today's money), the ground was built on the site of an earlier folly called Watkin's Tower. It was originally intended for the stadium to be demolished after the exhibition but instead was purchased by James White and then Arthur Elvin and continued to operate as a sporting and public event venue.

The first of 223 matches England men's senior would play at the 'original' Wembley Stadium took place on 12 April 1924 as the Three Lions drew 1-1 with Scotland in the British Home Championship.

In the summer of 1948, Wembley was used as the main venue for the Olympic Games where Dutch sprinter Fanny Blankers-Koen, decathlete Bob Mathias of the United States and Czech long-distance runner Emil Zátopek were among the notable gold medallists.

HALCYON DAYS

For the first 27 years of its existence, the only international matches hosted by England at Wembley Stadium were against Scotland. The first international team other than Scotland were Argentina, who the Three Lions beat 2-1 on 9 May 1951 thanks to goals from Stan Mortensen and Jackie Milburn.

The venue was particularly to the liking of Mortensen, who scored a hat-trick for Blackpool in their 1953 FA Cup final victory over Bolton Wanderers. Despite Mortensen's trio of goals, the game is forever known as the 'Matthews Final' in recognition of Blackpool winger Stanley Matthews' performance on the day, as he almost single-handedly turned the Tangerine's 3-1 deficit into a 4-3 win.

When Tottenham Hotspur won 2-0 against Leicester City in the FA Cup Final of 6 May

1961 at Wembley Stadium, Spurs became the first English side in the 20th century, to complete the 'double', as both league champions and FA Cup Winners that year. Four days later, England completed one of their biggest ever wins at Wembley, thrashing Mexico 8-0 in an international friendly. Bobby Charlton scored a hat-trick in the win while Bryan Douglas bagged a brace. Bobby Robson, Gerry Hitchens and Ron Flowers were also on target.

The Three Lions replicated that score line on 14 October 1987 against Turkey but secured their biggest Wembley victory five years earlier as they beat Luxembourg 9-0 on 15 December 1982

thanks to a Luther Blissett hat-trick, an own-goal and additional goals from Steve Coppell, Tony Woodcock, Mark Chamberlain, Glenn Hoddle and Phil Neal.

England's greatest footballing moment occurred at Wembley Stadium on 30 July 1966 as Sir Alf Ramsey's Three Lions beat West Germany 4-2 after extra-time in the FIFA World Cup Final. Geoff Hurst scored a hat-trick in the memorable final while Martin Peters was also on target. Wembley hosted all six of the Three Lions' matches during the tournament, including the 1-0 last-eight win over Argentina and the 2-1 triumph against Portugal in the semi-final.

A GLOBAL STAGE

The 'original' Wembley Stadium was used as a concert venue from the early 1970s onwards with Elton John, The Who, Bruce Springsteen, U2, Wham!, Queen, Genesis, Madonna, Michael Jackson, Pink Floyd, INXS, Guns N'Roses, Tina Turner and The Spice Girls amongst those artists to perform there. Arguably, the most famous concert at the old ground was the British leg of 'Live Aid' – a music-based fundraising initiative that took place on 13 July 1985. Around 72,000 spectators attended the Wembley event, watched by a global television audience in excess of 1.9 billion people.

Football came home in 1996 as England hosted that summer's UEFA European Championships. Terry Venables' Three Lions – who played all five of their tournament matches at Wembley - were in fine form. Highlights including a 2-0 win over Scotland, a 4-1 thrashing of the Netherlands and a penalty shootout victory over Spain in the quarter finals. They eventually lost an epic semi-final against Germany on penalties.

In November 1999, Wembley National Stadium Limited submitted a planning application to demolish the then-existing stadium and build a new, 90,000-seater venue. Planning permission was obtained the following year with Chelsea beating Aston Villa 1-0 in the stadium's last FA Cup Final on

20 May 2000 while England were defeated 1-0 by Germany in the last international there on 7 October 2000.

England's first senior international at the 'new' Wembley Stadium saw them draw 1-1 with Brazil on 1 June 2007 in front of a crowd of 88,745.

A NEW STADIUM FOR A NEW CENTURY

During the 2012 Summer Olympics, Wembley hosted six men's and three women's matches in the football tournament, including both finals.

England senior women's team attracted their record home crowd of 45,619 for a match against Germany at Wembley in 2014. On a return to the 'Home of Football' in 2019, for a clash against the same opponents, a new record crowd figure of 77,768 was set for a Lionesses home fixture.

The old Wembley Stadium was demolished between 2002 and 2003 and replaced by the current Wembley Stadium, which was opened in 2007. Designed by Populous and Foster and Partners, the venue features a 134-metre-high (440ft) arch, which supports over 75% of its roof load and is an iconic symbol for the venue – visible from many points across London.

The new stadium was completed and handed over to The Football Association on 9 March 2007. On the 24th of that month, a sell-out crowd – albeit one restricted in size to 55,700 – saw the first-ever official football match (with staff and charity games having previously taken place) to be staged at the venue, as England Under-21s hosted their counterparts from Italy. David Bentley, Wayne Routledge and Matt Derbyshire scored for the Young Lions in a 3-3 draw while Giampaolo Pazzini scored the venue's first hat-trick for the visitors.

Chelsea were 1-0 winners (after extra-time) in the stadium's first FA Cup Final while England drew 1-1 in its first senior international on 1 June 2007. Wembley Stadium hosted the UEFA Champions League final for the first time on 28 May 2011 when Barcelona played Manchester United and staged the showpiece occasion once again in 2013 and will do so again in 2024.

The delayed UEFA Euro 2020 saw eight tournament matches played at Wembley Stadium, including both semi-finals and the final. England featured in six of those games – including three group games against Croatia, Czech Republic and Scotland, a quarter-final against Germany and a semi-final against Denmark - as they reached the final of the competition, where they were beaten on penalties by Italy.

On 31 July 2020 a crowd of 87,192 - a record attendance for a women's international fixture in Europe and for any European Championship finals match – packed into Wembley Stadium for the UEFA Women's Euro 2022 Final between England and Germany. An extra-time winner from Chloe Kelly that day ensured the Lionesses their first major trophy success.

LEAH WILLIAMSON

CROSSWORD

Add the surnames of these current England players to complete this crossword.

Answers on pages 60-61.

ACROSS

1. The Lionesses' all-time record goalscorer - ELLEN _ _ _ _ _ (5)

2. Impressed on loan at Crystal Palace during the 2021/22 season - CONOR _ _ _ _ _ _ _ _ _ (9)

3. Scored her first four goals for England in the record 20-0 win v Latvia in November 2021 - LAUREN _ _ _ _ (4)

5. Centre-back who started his career with his hometown club Barnsley - JOHN _ _ _ _ _ _ (6)

9. England's number one goalkeeper at UEFA Euro 2020 - JORDAN _ _ _ _ _ _ _ _ (8)

10. Scored two of England's four goals in the 2022 Arnold Clarke Cup - MILLIE _ _ _ _ _ _ (6)

11. Nottingham-born goalkeeper who signed for Manchester United from Wolfsburg in 2019 - MARY _ _ _ _ _ (5)

DOWN

1. Captained the Lionesses against Kazakhstan in September 2018 - KIERA _ _ _ _ _ (5)

4. Midfielder who was loaned to Dutch club Vitesse and then-EFL Championship club, Derby County earlier in his career - MASON _ _ _ _ _ (5)

6. Scorer of a memorable free-kick against Croatia at the 2018 FIFA World Cup - KIERAN _ _ _ _ _ _ _ _ (8)

7. Scored her first international hat-trick against Northern Ireland in October 2021 - BETH _ _ _ _ (4)

8. Netted for England for the first time with brace against Iceland in November 2020 - PHIL _ _ _ _ _ (5)

GUESS THE GOALCORER

Can you remember who scored in the below games?

Answers on pages 60-61.

v SWITZERLAND - 26 MARCH 2022

v NORTH MACEDONIA - 08 APRIL 2022

v NORTHERN IRELAND - 12 APRIL 2022

v GERMANY - 07 JUNE 2022

ENGLAND AT THE 2022 FIFA WORLD CUP

GAME 1
MON 21 NOV 2022 • 1PM GMT
KHALIFA INTERNATIONAL
STADIUM, AL RAYYAN

☐ **ENGLAND**
☐ **IRAN**

GOALSCORERS

GAME 2
FRI 25 NOV 2022 • 7PM GMT
AHMAD BIN ALI STADIUM,
AL RAYYAN

☐ **ENGLAND**
☐ **UNITED STATES**

GOALSCORERS

GAME 3
TUES 29 NOV 2022 • 7PM GMT
AHMAD BIN ALI STADIUM,
AL RAYYAN

☐ **ENGLAND**
☐ **WALES**

GOALSCORERS

FINAL GROUP B TABLE

		P	W	D	L	GF	GA	GD	PTS
1	(Q)								
2	(Q)								
3									
4									

ROUND OF 16

DATE, TIME & VENUE

☐ GROUP A WINNER/RUNNER-UP
☐ OPPONENT

GOALSCORERS

QUARTER-FINAL

DATE, TIME & VENUE

☐ WINNER OF MATCH 49 OR 51
☐ OPPONENT

GOALSCORERS

SEMI-FINAL

DATE, TIME & VENUE

☐ WINNER OF MATCH 58 OR 59
☐ OPPONENT

GOALSCORERS

FINAL

FINALIST A ☐ **VS** ☐ FINALIST B

DATE, TIME & VENUE

GOALSCORERS

ANSWERS

WORDSEARCH Page 40

T	X	J	F	I	R	C	J	V	S
Y	C	N	R	A	M	S	E	Y	O
N	Z	P	X	R	R	L	G	V	U
S	E	U	O	G	W	M	P	R	T
R	A	V	R	W	S	L	T	E	H
O	N	M	I	U	E	S	A	A	G
B	A	T	P	L	J	L	Y	G	A
S	R	D	Q	S	L	H	L	A	T
O	K	S	I	R	O	E	O	N	E
N	H	J	W	T	E	N	R	E	L

QUIZ Page 42

1. Glasgow
2. Cuthbert Ottaway
3. Sylvia Gore
4. Hope Powell
5. Latvia
6. Aston Villa and Middlesbrough
7. 39 Steps
8. 2007
9. Germany
10. Italy
11. B – 75
12. Paul Nevin
13. Sarina Wiegman
14. Ellen White
15. Austria
16. Iran
17. Wales
18. St Mary's Stadium, Southampton
19. Peter Shilton
20. Fara Williams
21. UEFA Champions League final
22. Harry Kane
23. C – 21
24. Kyle Walker
25. Northern Ireland
26. Jordan Pickford
27. Barcelona
28. Sheffield
29. Bobby Charlton
30. Kyle Walker-Peters

WHO AM I?! Page 48

CROSSWORD Page 57

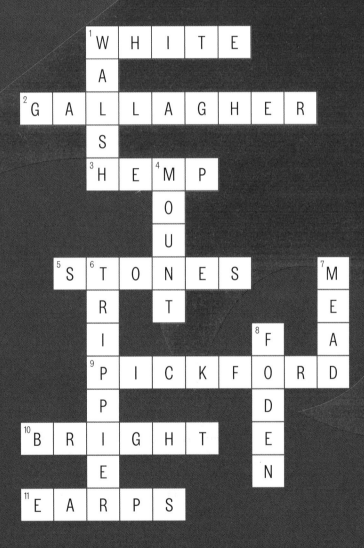

GUESS THE GOALSCORERS Page 58

SPOT THE PLAYERS

CAN YOU SPOT THE FIVE LIONS & FIVE LIONESSES HIDING IN THE CROWD?